# OLIVES

Happy 55TH!
To My Best Bud
Love,
Jeanne

Designed by Eddie Goldfine

Culinary editing by Tamar Zakut

Edited by Sorelle Weinstein

Photography by Danya Weiner

Layout by Michal Erez

Nutritional Information by Rachel Granot, B.S., M.P.H.

**Library of Congress Cataloging-in-Publication Data**

Laskin, Avner.

Olives : more than 70 delicious & healthy recipes / Avner Laskin ; photography by Danya Weiner.

p. cm.

Includes index.

ISBN-13: 978-1-4027-4468-6

ISBN-10: 1-4027-4468-4

1. Cookery (Olives) I. Title.


TX813.O4L37 2008

641.6'463--dc22                                         2007012953


2  4  6  8  10  9  7  5  3  1


Published by Sterling Publishing Co., Inc.

387 Park Avenue South, New York, NY 10016

© 2008 by Penn Publishing Ltd.

Distributed in Canada by Sterling Publishing

ᶜ/o Canadian Manda Group, 165 Dufferin Street,

Toronto, Ontario, Canada M6K 3H6

Distributed in the United Kingdom by GMC Distribution Services,

Castle Place, 166 High Street, Lewes, East Sussex, England BN7 1XU

Distributed in Australia by Capricorn Link (Australia) Pty. Ltd.

P.O. Box 704, Windsor, NSW 2756, Australia


*Printed in China*

Sterling ISBN-13: 978-1-4027-4468-6

ISBN-10: 1-4027-4468-4


For information about custom editions, special sales, premium and
corporate purchases, please contact Sterling Special Sales
Department at 800-805-5489 or specialsales@sterlingpub.com.

# AVNER LASKIN

# OLIVES

*More than 70 Delicious*
*& Healthy Recipes*

PHOTOGRAPHY BY DANYA WEINER

STERLING

New York / London
**www.sterlingpublishing.com**

TABLE OF CONTENTS

# ALL ABOUT OLIVES

## INTRODUCTION

Why write a cookbook about olives? Most people conjure up images of olives as a garnish in a good martini or a topping for pizza, but this versatile fruit should not be used merely as an afterthought. The olive deserves to take center stage in the theater of our kitchen productions. It deserves top billing on the marquees of our menus and, with its subtle flavor and wonderful aroma, the olive deserves recognition and appreciation as both a staple in Mediterranean cooking and a wonderful ingredient in any cuisine.

I live, work, and cook in the Mediterranean. I have been a professional chef for 20 years. I always knew about olives but I regarded them either as the progenitors of olive oil or in the capacity of being served pickled — sitting lonely in a small white dish on the table before a meal. When I began to research olives in cooking, however, I was amazed to find that olives are incredibly versatile and, as such, are appropriate for a range of dishes. Even the humble yet heavenly olive oil can be made somewhat less humble with the addition of herbs and spices (see "From the Pantry," page 10). Simple olives in a white dish can be transformed into delicious French Aperitif Olives (page 16) or fragrant Cracked Olives (page 18).

During the course of my research, I discovered so many recipes and such a wealth of background material that I decided to write a book to share it all with you. Before we begin cooking, let us turn our attention to the history and nature of this unique fruit.

The olive *(Olea europaea)* is a species of small tree native to coastal areas of the eastern Mediterranean region and the maritime regions of Asia Minor. The tree is a tough plant and is able to thrive in conditions of soil and climate that would easily kill less hardy plants. In fact, even if you cut down an olive tree, the stump will continue to blossom after the main part of the tree has been severed. The olive tree produces its fruit in the fall months when the weather in the region begins to cool and the days begin to shorten. The fruit of the olive tree is inedible when first harvested and must be treated to reduce its bitterness and make it palatable. Green olives are unripe olives which are allowed to ferment and pickle in brine or other solutions to make them edible. Black olives are ripe olives which can be pickled but are never allowed to ferment, which is why black olives usually have a milder flavor than their green-skinned siblings. As well as being a staple in Mediterranean cooking, the oil from olives has been used for centuries as lamp oil and in cosmetics, medicines, and soap.

*Olives* contains more than 70 recipes with olives as their main ingredient. In "For the Pantry," you will learn how to prepare flavored olive oils and various

olives and olive spreads which can be either served alone or used for other recipes. In "Vegetables and Salads," you will discover delicious recipes for fresh dishes which showcase olives with other garden delights. One of my favorite chapters is "Breads and Baked Goods." The heavenly aroma of baking bread and rising pastry dough will fill your house when you prepare these hearty recipes. In the chapter "Rice and Pasta," you will find recipes that will satisfy the carb-lover in you. The chapter "Fish and Seafood" boasts delectable recipes that will dazzle and tantalize your guests. Finally, in "Chicken and Meat," you will find some scrumptious and novel entrees, as well as interesting takes on classic dishes.

When following the recipes in this book, always remember to read through the entire recipe before you begin in order to familiarize yourself with the various ingredients and steps. As always, remember to have fun and feel free to experiment and use your own tastes as a guide. If you do, I guarantee that your recipes will be resounding successes and your palate will be properly pleased.

*Bon appetit!*

Avner Laskin

## NUTRITIONAL INFORMATION

The use of olives and olive oil in the Mediterranean diet has long been credited as a contributor to fewer instances of heart disease and strokes in countries where olives and olive oil are staples. Indeed, in research that was conducted after the second World War, the diets of Greece and Crete were found to be full of better, healthier nutritional choices than Western countries of similar size and demographics. What makes the Mediterranean diet so healthy? Simply put, the Mediterranean diet is rich in whole grains, fruits, and vegetables, and both olives and olive oil. Eighty percent of the fats in the Mediterranean diet comes from olives and olive oil, while in Western countries, most of the fats come from animal fats.

The fat in olive oil is monounsaturated fat and has been thought to increase the elasticity of the arterial walls and possibly help reduce the "bad" cholesterol in the body. Furthermore, olives are a good source of Vitamin E, which is an antioxidant and is thought to protect against the damaging effects of free radicals, which may contribute to the development of chronic diseases such as cancer. It has been further documented that olive oil intake bolsters the immune system against external attacks from microorganisms, bacteria, and viruses. Recent research has concluded that the fatty acids in the makeup of olive oil are good allies in lowering the amount of detrimental particles and disease-causing agents in the blood. The fatty acids in olive oil have also been reported to play an important part in various immune functions. They are involved in the regulation of the immune system in general. In short, though the full health benefits of olives and olive oil are only beginning to be explored, there is ample reason to include them as part of a healthful, nutritious diet.

When cooking with olive oil, it is important to know which oil to use. In recipes that call for cooking with hot oil, as in "Lamb Casserole with Black Olives" (page 116), it is enough to use "100% Pure Olive Oil." However, for use in salads or sauces where cold olive oil is called for, it is preferable to use "Extra-Virgin Olive Oil." Extra-virgin olive oil is oil which comes from the first pressing of the olives and contains no more than 0.8 percent acidity. It is a superior tasting oil.

When a recipe calls for a specific type of olive, such as Syrian or Spanish, these are recommended only as suggestions and it is certainly acceptable to substitute olives of similar size and/or taste to suit your own preference. When you begin to cook with olives, it is advisable to purchase them from gourmet shops that allow you to taste the olives before you buy them. Once you become familiar with the different varieties of olives, and know what you like, you can then purchase canned olives with confidence from any supermarket.

# FOR THE
# PANTRY

# FLAVORED OILS

*These wonderful flavored oils are essential ingredients to have handy for pasta sauces, salad dressings, or almost any recipe.*

## BLACK OLIVE OIL

### INGREDIENTS

*Makes 2 cups*

½ cup pitted black olives, pickled in salt

2 cups olive oil

½ teaspoon salt

### PREPARATION

1. Place the olives, half the olive oil, and salt in a food processor with a metal blade and process until smooth.

2. Transfer to an airtight container, add the remaining olive oil, and shake well before use.

3. Store the oil in the refrigerator for up to 1 month or store at room temperature. It is important that the container is closed tightly before storing.

## ANCHOVY FLAVORED OLIVE OIL

### INGREDIENTS

*Makes 2 cups*

¼ cup anchovies, filleted

2 cups olive oil

2 cloves garlic, chopped

### PREPARATION

1. Place the anchovies and half the olive oil in a small saucepan.

2. Heat the oil over low heat while stirring with a wooden spoon. Cook the oil until the anchovies are completely dissolved in the oil.

3. Remove from the heat and transfer to a food processor with a metal blade.

4. Add the remaining olive oil and garlic, and process until smooth.

5. Strain the mixture through a fine sieve and transfer to an airtight container.

6. Store the oil in the refrigerator for up to 1 month.

## BASIL FLAVORED OLIVE OIL

### INGREDIENTS

*Makes 2 cups*

2 cups olive oil

1 cup fresh basil

$\frac{1}{2}$ teaspoon salt

### PREPARATION

1. Heat half the olive oil in a small saucepan over medium heat until it reaches 220°F. You may need to use a candy thermometer to measure the temperature of the oil.

2. Add the basil, remove the oil from the heat, and cover.

3. Set aside for 20 minutes until cool.

4. Pour the oil and basil into a food processor with a metal blade.

5. Add the remaining 1 cup of olive oil and salt, and process until smooth.

6. Strain the mixture through a fine sieve and transfer to an airtight container.

7. Store the oil in the refrigerator for up to 1 month.


## LEMON-CHILI FLAVORED OLIVE OIL

### INGREDIENTS

*Makes 2 cups*

2 cups olive oil

2 red chili peppers and seeds, finely chopped

Peel of one lemon, finely grated

$\frac{1}{2}$ teaspoon salt

### PREPARATION

1. Heat half the olive oil in a small saucepan over medium heat until it reaches 220°F. You may need to use a candy thermometer to measure the temperature of the oil.

2. Add the chili peppers, remove the oil from the heat, and cover.

3. Set aside for 20 minutes to cool and add the grated lemon peel, salt, and the remaining oil.

4. Transfer to an airtight container.

5. Store the oil in the refrigerator for up to 1 month.

*(see photo on page 15)*


## OLIVE OIL WITH ROSEMARY

### INGREDIENTS

*Makes 2 cups*

2 cups olive oil

$\frac{1}{4}$ cup fresh rosemary

$\frac{1}{2}$ teaspoon salt

### PREPARATION

1. Heat half the olive oil in a small saucepan over medium heat until it reaches 220°F. You may need to use a candy thermometer to measure the temperature of the oil.

2. Add the rosemary, remove the oil from the heat, and cover.

3. Set aside for 20 minutes until cool.

4. Pour the oil and rosemary into a food processor with a metal blade.

5. Add the remaining olive oil and salt, and process for 2 minutes.

6. Strain the mixture through a fine sieve and transfer to an airtight container.

7. Store the oil in the refrigerator for up to 1 month.

*(see photo on page 15)*

## OLIVE OIL WITH OREGANO

### INGREDIENTS

*Makes 2 cups*

2 cups olive oil

⅓ cup fresh oregano

½ teaspoon salt

### PREPARATION

1. Heat half the olive oil in a small saucepan over medium heat until it reaches 220°F. You may need to use a candy thermometer to measure the temperature of the oil.

2. Add the oregano, remove the oil from the heat, and cover.

3. Set aside for 20 minutes until cool.

4. Pour the oil and oregano into a food processor with a metal blade.

5. Add the remaining olive oil and salt, and process for 2 minutes.

6. Strain the mixture through a fine sieve and transfer to an airtight container.

7. Store the oil in the refrigerator for up to 1 month.

## TOMATO CONFIT FLAVORED OLIVE OIL

### INGREDIENTS

*Makes 3 cups*

Bowl of ice water

10 fresh tomatoes, blanched

3 sprigs fresh thyme

2 sprigs rosemary

3 cloves garlic, peeled and halved lengthwise

½ teaspoon salt

2 cups olive oil

### PREPARATION

1. Preheat oven to 275°F.

2. Fill a medium saucepan with water and bring to a boil. When the water is boiling, add the tomatoes.

3. Boil the tomatoes for 30 seconds. Remove the tomatoes from the water and transfer immediately to a bowl of ice water.

4. Peel the tomatoes, remove the seeds, and cut into quarters.

5. Arrange the tomato quarters in a 2-inch-deep pan.

6. Place the thyme, rosemary, and garlic in the pan around the tomatoes.

7. Sprinkle salt over the pan and pour the olive oil over all the ingredients.

8. Bake for 1½–2 hours until the tomatoes have shrunk and turned a dark color. The longer the tomatoes remain in the oven, the richer the flavor of the final oil will be.

9. Remove the tomatoes from the oven and transfer to a food processor with a metal blade.

10. Process the mixture until smooth.

11. Transfer to an airtight container and refrigerate.

12. Store the oil in the refrigerator for up to 1 month.

*Opposite (from left to right): Lemon-Chili Flavored Olive Oil, Olive Oil with Rosemary, Olive Oil with Oregano, Tomato Confit Flavored Olive Oil*

# SPICED OLIVES

*Spiced olives are also an essential ingredient to have on hand when making pasta, sauces, salads, or any dish.*

## FRENCH APERITIF OLIVES

### INGREDIENTS

*Makes 2 cups*

1 pound green olives, Syrian or Spanish

3 tablespoons Herbes de Provence*

1 teaspoon fresh thyme*

1 teaspoon fresh oregano*

4 tablespoons extra-virgin olive oil

1 tablespoon coarse black pepper

* You may use dried herbs if you cannot find fresh.

*Opposite (from left to right): French Aperitif Olives and North African Spiced Olives*

### PREPARATION

1. Place all the ingredients in a bowl and mix well.

2. Transfer to an airtight container and refrigerate for up to 3 hours.

3. Store the olives in the refrigerator for up to 2 weeks.

## NORTH AFRICAN SPICED OLIVES

### INGREDIENTS

*Makes 2 cups*

1 pound green olives, Syrian or Spanish

1 lemon, sliced into $\frac{1}{3}$-inch slices

1 tablespoon sweet paprika

2 red chili peppers, finely chopped

### PREPARATION

1. Place all the ingredients in a bowl and mix well.

2. Transfer to an airtight container and refrigerate for up to 24 hours.

3. Store the olives in the refrigerator for up to 2 weeks.

# CAJUN OLIVES

## INGREDIENTS

*Makes 2 cups*

1 pound green olives, Syrian or Spanish

1 tablespoon Old Bay Seasoning (available in most groceries)

1 tablespoon smoked paprika

1 teaspoon garlic powder

## PREPARATION

1. Place all the ingredients in a bowl and mix well.

2. Transfer to an airtight container and refrigerate for 24 hours.

3. Serve after chilling for 24 hours or store for up to 2 weeks in the refrigerator.

*Opposite: Cracked Olives*

# CRACKED OLIVES

## INGREDIENTS

*Makes 2 cups*

1 pound cracked green olives

3 celery stalks, finely sliced

1 white onion, finely chopped

2 cloves garlic, finely chopped

1 cup olive oil

3 tablespoons white wine vinegar

## PREPARATION

1. Place all the ingredients in a bowl and mix well.

2. Transfer to an airtight container and refrigerate for up to 24 hours.

3. Store the olives in the refrigerator for up to 2 weeks.

# SPICED KALAMATA OLIVES

## INGREDIENTS

*Makes 2 cups*

1 pound Kalamata olives, liquid drained

2 tablespoons balsamic vinegar

2 tablespoons olive oil

1 teaspoon ground black pepper

2 cloves garlic, chopped

1 teaspoon fresh lemon zest

## PREPARATION

1. Place all the ingredients in a bowl and mix well.

2. Transfer to an airtight container and refrigerate for 24 hours.

3. Serve after chilling for 24 hours or store for up to 2 weeks in the refrigerator.

*Opposite: Marinated Olives with Celery and Onions*

# MARINATED OLIVES WITH CELERY AND ONIONS

## INGREDIENTS

*Makes 2 cups*

1 pound green olives, Syrian or Spanish

2 red chili peppers, thinly sliced, with seeds

3 stalks celery, thinly sliced

$\frac{1}{4}$ cup white onion, finely chopped

2 cloves garlic, thinly sliced

1 cup olive oil

1 tablespoon fresh rosemary

3 tablespoons white wine vinegar

## PREPARATION

1. Place all the ingredients in a bowl and mix well.

2. Transfer to an airtight container and refrigerate for 24 hours.

3. After chilling for 24 hours, serve or store in the refrigerator for up to 2 weeks.

# SPREADS

*These tasty spreads are wonderful on sandwiches, on toast, or as dips for crusty fresh bread.*
*Prepare them in advance and use them to liven up chicken, fish, and pasta recipes.*

## OLIVES WITH PICKLED LEMONS

### INGREDIENTS

*Makes 3 cups*

1 cup pitted green olives

2/3 cup pickled lemons (these may be purchased in specialty shops or online)

2 cloves garlic

1/2 teaspoon salt

1/2 teaspoon sweet paprika

1 cup olive oil

### PREPARATION

1. Place all the ingredients except for half the oil in a food processor with a metal blade. Process the ingredients.

2. While processing, gradually add the remaining olive oil. Process until smooth.

3. Transfer to an airtight container and refrigerate for up to 1 month.

## OLIVE AND BAKED GARLIC SPREAD

### INGREDIENTS

*Makes 2 cups*

12 cloves garlic, peeled

1 cup olive oil

1/2 cup pitted black olives

1/2 teaspoon salt

1/2 teaspoon ground black pepper

### PREPARATION

1. Preheat the oven to 375°F.

2. Place the garlic cloves in a heat-proof dish and pour the olive oil over all the garlic. Be sure the garlic is well coated with oil.

3. Bake for 40 minutes.

4. Remove from the oven and set aside for 30 minutes until cool.

5. Remove the garlic from the dish using a slotted spoon and transfer to a food processor with a metal blade. Set the oil aside. Add the olives, salt, and pepper, and process.

6. While processing, gradually add the olive oil which was in the dish with the garlic. Process until smooth.

7. Transfer to an airtight container. Store it in the refrigerator for up to 5 days.

# OLIVE SALSA WITH BASIL AND ANCHOVIES

## INGREDIENTS

*Makes 1 cup*

1/2 cup pitted black olives, finely chopped

3 tablespoons balsamic vinegar

4 tablespoons basil, finely chopped

1/2 teaspoon salt

1/2 teaspoon ground black pepper

1/2 cup Anchovy Flavored Olive Oil (page 12)

## PREPARATION

1. Place all the ingredients except for half the oil in a large bowl and mix well.

2. Gradually add the remaining olive oil while stirring.

3. Transfer to an airtight container. Store it in the refrigerator for up to 5 days.

# OLIVE OIL AND LEMON MAYONNAISE

## INGREDIENTS

*Makes 2 cups*

3 medium ripe lemons, cut in half lengthwise

2 cups water

2 tablespoons coarse salt

1/4 cup sugar

1/3 cup pitted black olives

1 clove garlic

1 cup olive oil

## PREPARATION

1. Place the lemons, water, salt, and sugar in a small saucepan.

2. Bring to a boil over medium heat.

3. Lower the heat and simmer for 45 minutes until the lemon peels are soft.

4. Using a slotted spoon, remove the lemons from the water and transfer them to a bowl. Set aside the cooking water.

5. Allow the lemons to cool completely. You may place the lemons in the freezer to cool them more rapidly if you are pressed for time.

6. Place the olives, lemons, and garlic in a food processor with a metal blade and process. While processing, gradually add a tablespoon of the cooking water and the olive oil and continue to process until the mixture is smooth and uniform and has a texture similar to mayonnaise.

7. Transfer to an airtight container. Store it in the refrigerator for up to 2 days.

# GREEN OLIVE AIOLI

## INGREDIENTS

*Makes 2 cups*

1 medium potato

3 cloves garlic

1/2 cup pitted green olives

4 egg yolks

1 cup olive oil

Juice of 1 medium lemon

1/2 teaspoon salt

## PREPARATION

1. Preheat the oven to 400°F.

2. Wrap the potato in aluminum foil and bake in the oven for 45 minutes or until completely soft.

3. Remove the potato from the oven, peel, and transfer to the freezer for 30 minutes, or until completely cool.

4. Place the potato in a food processor with a metal blade. Add the garlic and olives and process.

5. While processing the mixture, gradually add the egg yolks and then gradually add half the olive oil.

6. Alternate between adding the remaining olive oil and the lemon juice while processing the mixture. The mixture should resemble mayonnaise in consistency and have a yellow-green tint. If the mixture is too thick, add more lemon juice. If the mixture is too thin, add more egg yolk.

7. Add the salt and any remaining olive oil and lemon juice. Process for 1 more minute or until the mixture is smooth.

8. Transfer to an airtight container. Store it in the refrigerator for up to 2 days.

# OLIVE PESTO

## INGREDIENTS

*Makes 2 cups*

1/2 cup pitted green olives

1 cup fresh basil leaves

3 tablespoons pine nuts

2 cloves garlic

1 teaspoon salt

1/4 cup grated Parmesan cheese

1 cup olive oil

## PREPARATION

1. Place all the ingredients except half the olive oil in a food processor with a metal blade.

2. Process the ingredients and gradually add the remaining olive oil while processing.

3. Transfer the mixture to an airtight container. Store it in the refrigerator for up to 1 week or freeze for up to 3 weeks.

*Opposite: Olive Pesto*

# BLACK OLIVE TAPENADE

## INGREDIENTS

*Makes 2 cups*

1 cup pitted black olives

2 cloves garlic

3 anchovies in brine, filleted

2 tablespoons fresh thyme leaves

1 cup olive oil

## PREPARATION

1. Place all the ingredients except half the olive oil in a food processor with a metal blade and process until smooth.

2. While processing, gradually add the remaining olive oil.

3. Transfer to an airtight container. Store it in the refrigerator for up to 1 month.

*Opposite: Green Olive Tapenade*

# SPICY OLIVE SALSA

## INGREDIENTS

*Makes 1 cups*

2 hot red chili peppers, finely chopped

1/2 cup pitted green olives, finely chopped

1/4 cup fresh parsley, finely chopped

2 cloves garlic, finely chopped

1 tablespoon coriander, chopped

1/2 teaspoon salt

2 tablespoons red wine vinegar

1/2 cup olive oil

## PREPARATION

1. Place the chili peppers, olives, parsley, garlic, and coriander in a bowl and mix well.

2. Add the salt, mix well, and set aside for 15 minutes.

3. Add the vinegar. Gradually add the olive oil while mixing.

4. Transfer to an airtight container. Store it in the refrigerator for up to 2 days.

# GREEN OLIVE TAPENADE

## INGREDIENTS

*Makes 2 cups*

1 cup pitted green olives

2 cloves garlic

2 tablespoons fresh thyme leaves

1 cup olive oil

## PREPARATION

1. Place all the ingredients except for half the olive oil in a food processor with a metal blade. Process the ingredients.

2. While processing, gradually add the remaining olive oil. Process until smooth.

3. Transfer to an airtight container. Store it in the refrigerator for up to 1 month.

## OLIVE AND GOAT CHEESE SPREAD

### INGREDIENTS

*Makes 2 cups*

1 cup pitted green olives

½ pound fresh goat cheese

¼ cup olive oil

1 tablespoon fresh basil

1 tablespoon fresh parsley, chopped

½ tablespoon lemon juice, freshly squeezed

2 cloves garlic

### PREPARATION

1. Place all the ingredients except for half the olive oil in a food processor with a metal blade. Process until the mixture is thick and creamy.

2. Gradually add the remaining olive oil while processing.

3. Transfer to an airtight container and serve or store in the refrigerator for up to 3 days.

*Opposite: Olives with Sun-Dried Tomatoes*

## KALAMATA OLIVES WITH AVOCADO

### INGREDIENTS

*Makes 2 cups*

1 cup pitted Kalamata olives

2 ripe medium avocados, peeled, seeded, and halved

¼ cup olive oil

½ teaspoon salt

1 tablespoon fresh coriander, chopped

½ tablespoon fresh lemon juice

2 cloves garlic

### PREPARATION

1. Place all the ingredients except for half the olive oil in a food processor with a metal blade. Process until the mixture is thick and creamy.

2. Gradually add the remaining olive oil while processing.

3. Transfer to an airtight container and serve or store in the refrigerator for up to 3 days.

## OLIVES WITH SUN-DRIED TOMATOES

### INGREDIENTS

*Makes 2½ cups*

1 cup pitted black olives

½ cup sun-dried tomatoes in olive oil

1 tablespoon fresh oregano

2 cloves garlic

1 cup olive oil

### PREPARATION

1. Place all the ingredients except for half the olive oil in a food processor with a metal blade. Process the ingredients.

2. While processing, gradually add the remaining olive oil. Process until smooth.

3. Transfer to an airtight container. Store it in the refrigerator for up to 1 month.

# VEGETABLES AND SALADS

# ARTICHOKE HEART AND OLIVE SALAD

*When trimming the artichokes, wear surgical gloves, as the oils will work into your hands and under your nails, making everything you touch taste bitter.*

## INGREDIENTS

*Serves 4*

5 fresh medium artichokes, with leaves

1 tablespoon coarse salt

Juice of 1 lemon

1/3 cup pitted black olives

1/2 cup cherry tomatoes, halved

1/4 cup parsley

1 small red onion, thinly sliced

1/2 teaspoon table salt

1/2 teaspoon ground black pepper

4 tablespoons olive oil

## PREPARATION

1. Cut the artichokes into two equal halves. Place them in a saucepan and cover with water. Add the coarse salt and 1 tablespoon of lemon juice. Bring to a boil over medium heat.

2. Reduce heat and cook for 20 minutes.

3. Remove from heat and transfer the artichokes to a large bowl. Pour cold water over the artichokes to prevent further cooking.

4. Use a sharp knife to trim the artichoke leaves so that only the soft leaves near the hearts remain. Remove any hairs from the artichoke hearts.

5. Transfer the cleaned and trimmed hearts to a clean bowl.

6. Add the olives, cherry tomatoes, parsley, red onion, table salt, and pepper, and mix well.

7. Add the olive oil and the remaining lemon juice and mix well. Let the salad stand for 30 minutes before serving. Store the salad at room temperature for up to 3 hours.

# ROASTED EGGPLANT AND OLIVE SALAD

*Rich roasted eggplant, piquant pesto, and tangy balsamic vinegar provide fabulous contrasting flavors in this recipe.*

## INGREDIENTS

*Serves 4*

2 medium eggplants, sliced widthwise into $\frac{1}{2}$-inch slices

$\frac{1}{4}$ cup olive oil, for the eggplant

1 teaspoon coarse salt

3 tablespoons Olive Pesto (page 24)

1 red onion, finely chopped

$\frac{1}{2}$ teaspoon table salt

$\frac{1}{2}$ teaspoon ground white pepper

2 tablespoons balsamic vinegar

$\frac{1}{4}$ cup olive oil, for the dressing

$\frac{1}{2}$ cup pitted black olives

$\frac{1}{2}$ cup cherry tomatoes, halved

## PREPARATION

1. Preheat the oven to 400°F.

2. Arrange the eggplant slices on a baking sheet and brush them with $\frac{1}{4}$ cup of olive oil. Sprinkle the coarse salt on top and bake for 20 minutes or until golden brown.

3. While the eggplant is cooking, place the pesto, red onion, table salt, pepper, and balsamic vinegar into a large bowl, and mix well with a fork.

4. Gradually add the olive oil while stirring the dressing. Mix well.

5. Remove the eggplant from the oven and transfer to the bowl with the dressing while still warm.

6. Add the olives and cherry tomatoes and mix well.

7. Let stand for 30 minutes and serve at room temperature. Store the salad in the refrigerator for up to 2 days.

# POTATO SALAD WITH OLIVES

*This light and zesty potato salad is excellent when served as an accompaniment to a light lunch or Sunday brunch.*

## INGREDIENTS

*Serves 6*

2 pounds new potatoes, halved

$\frac{1}{4}$ cup Green Olive Tapenade (page 26)

2 tablespoons parsley, chopped

$\frac{1}{2}$ teaspoon salt

$\frac{1}{2}$ teaspoon white pepper

3 tablespoons red wine vinegar

$\frac{1}{4}$ cup olive oil

$\frac{1}{2}$ cup pitted black olives

$\frac{1}{2}$ cup cherry tomatoes, quartered

## PREPARATION

1. Place the potatoes in a large pan filled with water so that the water covers all the potatoes. Cook for 30 minutes over medium heat until the potatoes are soft.

2. While the potatoes are cooking, place the tapenade in a bowl. Add the parsley, salt, pepper, and vinegar, and mix well.

3. Gradually add the olive oil while stirring. Mix until you achieve a thick sauce. Set aside.

4. Once the potatoes have cooked, drain the water from the pot. While the potatoes are still warm, transfer to a large bowl.

5. Add the olives, cherry tomatoes, and the sauce prepared earlier.

6. Mix the salad well and set aside for 30 minutes before serving. Store the salad for up to 3 hours at room temperature before serving.

# GREEN SALAD WITH OLIVES AND PECORINO CHEESE

*Kalamata (or Calamata) olives are dark eggplant-colored Greek olives with a rich and fruity flavor. They are usually packed in olive oil or vinegar and are often slit so they absorb the flavor of the marinade.*

## INGREDIENTS

*Serves 4*

¼ cup olive oil

1 tablespoon Dijon-style mustard

2 tablespoons white wine vinegar

½ teaspoon salt

½ teaspoon ground white pepper

2 heads romaine lettuce

⅓ cup whole Kalamata olives

4 ounces hard pecorino cheese

## PREPARATION

1. Place the oil, mustard, vinegar, salt, and pepper in an airtight container, close the container, and shake well for at least 1 minute to mix the ingredients. The mixture should resemble a thick vinaigrette dressing.

2. Arrange the lettuce leaves on a serving platter and sprinkle the olives on top.

3. Use a sharp knife, vegetable peeler, or cheese slicer to slice the cheese into thin slices and arrange on top of the salad.

4. Drizzle the dressing over the salad using a spoon and serve immediately.

# GREEN BEAN AND OLIVE SALAD

*The combination of green beans and olives in this colorful salad make it a terrific summer treat.*

## INGREDIENTS

*Serves 4*

6 cups water

1 tablespoon coarse salt

1 pound fresh green beans (you may use frozen beans instead)

⅓ cup Olives with Sun-Dried Tomatoes (page 28)

½ tablespoon red wine vinegar

½ teaspoon table salt

½ teaspoon ground white pepper

¼ cup olive oil

½ cup cherry tomatoes, cut into quarters

½ cup pitted purple olives in wine, halved

## PREPARATION

1. Pour the water into a medium saucepan and add the coarse salt. Bring the water to a boil and add the green beans. Reduce heat and cook for 5 minutes.

2. While the beans are cooking, prepare the dressing. Place the olive spread, vinegar, table salt, pepper, and olive oil in a large bowl and mix well.

3. When the beans have finished cooking, drain them and transfer while still warm to the bowl with the dressing.

4. Add the cherry tomatoes and olives and mix well to coat all the ingredients with the dressing. Let stand for at least 30 minutes before serving at room temperature.

5. You may also store the salad for up to 3 hours at room temperature.

# TOMATOES STUFFED WITH SPICED OLIVES

*If your tomatoes do not stand upright, slice a small round from the bottom to create a flat base.*

## INGREDIENTS

*Serves 4*

8 ripe medium tomatoes

1/2 cup pitted green olives, chopped

1 cup steamed white rice (may be prepared ahead of time)

3 tablespoons olive oil

1 tablespoon Olive Pesto (page 24)

1 tablespoon fresh thyme

1 tablespoon fresh basil, chopped

2 tablespoons breadcrumbs

1/2 teaspoon salt

1/2 teaspoon ground black pepper

1 clove garlic, chopped

## PREPARATION

1. Preheat the oven to 400°F.

2. Use a sharp knife to cut the tops off the tomatoes and scoop out the insides to form small bowls.

3. Place the other ingredients in a medium bowl and mix well using a large spoon.

4. Spoon the filling mixture into each tomato. Use a generous amount of filling for each tomato so that the filling comes to just above the top of the tomato.

5. Place the stuffed tomatoes in a deep heat-proof dish.

6. Bake for 30 minutes.

7. Serve immediately. Store the tomatoes in the refrigerator for up to 2 days and reheat before serving.

# POTATO AND OLIVE GRATIN

*Many cooks believe that a gratin must contain cheese, but traditional French chefs often prepare gratin with a rich and creamy béchamel sauce.*

## INGREDIENTS

*Serves 6*

1 tablespoon olive oil

8 large potatoes, peeled and cut into ¼-inch-thick slices

½ cup pitted black olives, finely chopped

½ pound sweet cream

4 ounces butter

1 teaspoon salt

1 teaspoon ground white pepper

## PREPARATION

1. Grease a deep baking dish with the olive oil.

2. Place the potato slices in a single layer on the bottom of the pan. Sprinkle half the olives over the potatoes.

3. Place another layer of potatoes over the olives and sprinkle on the remaining olives. Place any remaining potatoes on top. Set aside.

4. Preheat the oven to 400°F.

5. Place the cream, butter, salt, and pepper in a small saucepan and bring to a boil over low heat.

6. Pour the sauce evenly over the potatoes.

7. Cover the baking dish with aluminum foil and bake in the oven for 45 minutes.

8. Remove the aluminum foil and return to the oven for another 15 minutes uncovered or until the top is golden brown.

9. Serve immediately or store the gratin in an airtight container in the refrigerator for up to 2 days. Reheat before serving.

# VEGETABLE AND OLIVE RATATOUILLE

*The word "ratatouille" appears to derive from the French word* tatouiller, *meaning "to stir," although the "rat" part may have derived from French army slang for chunky stew.*

## INGREDIENTS

*Serves 4*

2 carrots

1 orange pepper

2 medium yellow squash

1 yellow pepper

1 red pepper

3 celery stalks

1 white onion

1 medium eggplant

1½ cups olive oil

½ cup pitted black olives, halved

¼ cup tomato juice

2 tablespoons thyme

1 teaspoon salt

1 teaspoon ground black pepper

2 cloves garlic, finely chopped

## PREPARATION

1. Use a sharp knife to chop all the vegetables into ¼-inch pieces. Place each vegetable in a separate bowl.

2. Heat half the olive oil in a heavy skillet.

3. Sauté the carrots until they are golden. Transfer to a strainer and save the oil to sauté the next vegetable.

4. Sauté the rest of the vegetables in the same manner as the carrots, in this order: orange pepper, squash, yellow pepper, red pepper, celery, white onion, and finally eggplant. Remember to use the same oil for each vegetable and add more olive oil as needed.

5. Transfer all cooked vegetables to a large bowl.

6. Add the olives, tomato juice, thyme, salt, pepper, and garlic and mix well. Let stand for 30 minutes before serving.

7. Store the ratatouille in an airtight container in the refrigerator up to 2 days. Reheat before serving.

# ASPARAGUS IN OLIVE DRESSING

*Simple and elegant, this beautiful salad is a special addition to any meal.*

## INGREDIENTS

*Serves 4*

1 tablespoon coarse salt

½ cup pitted black olives, finely chopped

3 tablespoons olive oil

1 tablespoon balsamic vinegar

1 pound fresh green asparagus

## PREPARATION

1. Fill a large pot with water and add the coarse salt. Bring to a boil.

2. Meanwhile, place the olives, olive oil, and balsamic vinegar in a small bowl and mix well.

3. Cook the asparagus for 6 minutes in the boiling water.

4. Remove the asparagus from the water and shake off any excess water. Arrange the asparagus on a serving plate.

5. Spoon the dressing over the asparagus evenly and serve immediately.

6. Store the cooked asparagus in ice water in the refrigerator for up to 2 days. Store the dressing in an airtight container in the refrigerator for up to 4 days.

# WARM OLIVE SALAD

*For the tastiest salad, use large black Greek olives.*

## INGREDIENTS

*Serves 4*

2 tablespoons olive oil

1 medium white onion, finely chopped

3 cloves garlic, finely chopped

4 celery stalks, thinly sliced

2 cups pitted black olives

1 tablespoon thyme

1 teaspoon salt

$\frac{1}{2}$ teaspoon ground black pepper

2 tomatoes, cooked, peeled and cut into $\frac{1}{2}$-inch cubes

1 cup cherry tomatoes, cut into quarters

## PREPARATION

1. Place the olive oil, onion, garlic, and celery in a large skillet over high heat. Sauté for 4 minutes while stirring.

2. Add the olives, thyme, salt, pepper, and tomatoes, and continue to cook for 3 more minutes while stirring.

3. Add the cherry tomatoes and cook for another 4 minutes while stirring.

4. Serve immediately.

# TOMATO AND OLIVE SHAKSHUKA

*Shakshuka is a North African dish with many variations. This recipe is enhanced with scrumptious black olives.*

## INGREDIENTS

*Serves 4*

1 medium onion, finely chopped

1 red pepper, cut into $\frac{1}{4}$-inch cubes

2 cloves garlic, finely chopped

1 tablespoon olive oil

One 15-ounce can crushed tomatoes

1 tablespoon sweet paprika

$\frac{1}{2}$ teaspoon cayenne pepper

$1\frac{1}{2}$ teaspoons salt

$\frac{1}{2}$ cup pitted black olives, broken into pieces

4 large eggs

## PREPARATION

1. Place the onion, red pepper, garlic, and olive oil in a large heavy skillet over low heat and sauté until the vegetables are very soft.

2. Add the crushed tomatoes, paprika, cayenne pepper, and salt.

3. Cook over low heat for 40 minutes until the sauce is very thick.

4. Add the olives and mix well.

5. Crack the eggs gently and arrange them side-by-side on top of the mixture. Continue to cook over low heat for 20 minutes. Serve immediately.

6. You may prepare the sauce with the olives up to 2 days before and store in the refrigerator. Reheat the sauce before you add the eggs. You may also prepare this recipe in individual servings as shown in the photo. To do this, simply quarter the tomato mixture before cooking and place 1 egg in each serving.

# SPINACH SHAKSHUKA WITH OLIVES AND FETA CHEESE

*This is a novel variation on the traditional tomato-based shakshuka. The spinach, olives, and feta cheese lend a Turkish flavor to this breakfast dish.*

## INGREDIENTS

*Serves 2*

1 cup leeks, thinly sliced

¼ cup olive oil

1 cup chard, finely chopped

1 teaspoon salt

½ pound spinach, coarsely chopped

1 cup pitted green olives

1 tablespoon fresh lemon juice

1 tablespoon soy sauce

2 eggs

½ pound feta cheese

## PREPARATION

1. Place the leeks and olive oil in a large skillet and sauté over low heat for 3 minutes.

2. Add the chard and salt and mix well. Continue to cook over low heat for 15 minutes.

3. Add the spinach, olives, lemon juice, and soy sauce, and mix well. Cover the skillet and cook for 5 minutes.

4. Uncover the skillet. Crack the eggs gently and arrange them side-by-side on top of the mixture. Continue to cook over low heat for 20 minutes.

5. Crumble the feta cheese over the mixture, remove from heat, and serve immediately.

6. You may prepare the sauce up to 2 days in advance and store it in the refrigerator. Reheat the sauce before cooking the eggs and serving. You may also prepare this recipe in individual servings.

# BREADS
# AND
# BAKED
# GOODS

# RYE BREAD WITH BLACK OLIVES

*Served warm, thick, and crusty, this delicious country bread is the perfect accompaniment to pasta.*

## INGREDIENTS

*Serves 4*

1 tablespoon dried yeast

¾ cup cold water

1½ cups bread flour

1½ cups rye flour

⅔ cup pitted black olives

1 teaspoon salt

Flour for dusting

## PREPARATION

1. Place the yeast, water, bread flour, rye flour, and olives in a mixing bowl. Use an electric mixer with a kneading hook to mix the dough on low speed for 3 minutes.

2. Add the salt while kneading. Increase the mixing speed and continue to knead for 6 minutes.

3. Transfer the dough to a floured bowl, cover with a towel, and let stand to rise at room temperature for 1 hour, until the dough doubles in size.

4. After the dough has risen, transfer it to a floured work surface and form a ball.

5. Place a well-floured kitchen towel in the bottom of a bowl and place the ball of dough in the bowl to rise. Let stand at room temperature until the ball has doubled.

6. While the dough is rising, place a baking or pizza stone in the oven and preheat the oven to 420°F.

7. After the dough has risen, carefully turn it onto a floured work surface and form a loaf shape with your hands. Use a sharp knife to score 3 parallel lines on top of the loaf. Then swivel the loaf and score 3 more parallel lines. This will form diamonds or squares on top.

8. Transfer the dough to the baking stone and bake for 30 minutes.

9. The bread is ready when tapping on the bottom produces a hollow sound. Store the bread in an airtight container at room temperature for up to 2 days. If you wish to store the bread longer, you may put it in the freezer in a sealed freezer bag for up to 1 week. To reheat, defrost at room temperature and place in a 400°F oven for 6 minutes.

# ONION AND OLIVE BREAD

*Great-tasting and beautifully presented, this bread can accompany your next picnic and give the ants something to talk about.*

## INGREDIENTS

*Serves 4*

For the dough:

1/3 cup cold water

1/4 cup milk

1 tablespoon sugar

2 large eggs

1 tablespoon dried yeast

3 cups bread flour

2 tablespoons olive oil

2 teaspoons salt

Flour for dusting

For the onion topping:

1 tablespoon olive oil

1 pound onions, thinly sliced

1 teaspoon crushed garlic

2 tablespoons fresh thyme

1 1/4 cup anchovy fillets in oil, drained

1/4 cup pitted black olives

## PREPARATION

1. Place the water, milk, sugar, eggs, yeast, bread flour, and olive oil in a mixing bowl. Use an electric mixer with a kneading hook to mix the dough on low speed for 3 minutes.

2. Add the salt while kneading. Increase the mixing speed and continue to knead for 6 minutes.

3. Transfer the dough to a floured bowl, cover with a towel, and let stand to rise at room temperature for 1 hour, until the dough doubles in size.

4. To prepare the onion mixture, heat the olive oil in a large skillet over low heat. Add the onions, garlic, and thyme, and sauté while stirring.

5. Cook for 40–50 minutes until the mixture is golden brown. Remove from heat and set aside to cool.

6. When the dough has risen, transfer it to a floured work surface and divide it into 2 equal portions. Roll each portion of dough into a ball.

7. Use a floured rolling pin to gently roll each ball of dough into a 12-inch-long ellipse, 1/2-inch thick.

8. Sprinkle the onion topping evenly over each portion of dough.

9. Place a baking or pizza stone in the oven and preheat the oven to 450°F.

10. Carefully transfer one portion of dough to the hot baking stone and bake for 18 minutes. Remove the bread and bake the second portion.

11. Serve hot. You may put the bread in an airtight container at room temperature for up to 2 days. If you wish to store the bread longer, you may put it in the freezer in a sealed freezer bag for up to 1 week. To reheat, defrost at room temperature and place in a 400°F oven for 6 minutes.

# ITALIAN OLIVE BREAD

*Serve with a fresh garden salad for a delicious Sunday brunch.*

## INGREDIENTS

*Serves 4*

1 cup cold water

1 tablespoon dried yeast

3 cups bread flour

3 tablespoons olive oil

⅔ cup pitted green olives

1 teaspoon salt

Flour for dusting

## PREPARATION

1. Place the water, yeast, bread flour, olive oil, and olives in a mixing bowl. Use an electric mixer with a kneading hook to mix the dough on low speed for 3 minutes.

2. Add the salt while kneading. Increase the mixing speed and continue to knead for 8 minutes.

3. Transfer the dough to a floured bowl, cover with a towel, and let stand to rise at room temperature for 1 hour, until the dough doubles in size.

4. After the dough has risen, transfer to a floured work surface and form a ball of dough.

5. Place a well-floured kitchen towel in the bottom of a bowl and place the ball of dough in the bowl to rise. Let stand at room temperature until the ball has doubled in size.

6. While the dough is rising, place a baking or pizza stone in the oven and preheat the oven to 450°F.

7. After the dough has risen, carefully turn it onto a floured work surface and form a loaf shape with your hands. Use a sharp knife to score a line across the top of the loaf. Then swivel the loaf and score another line perpendicular to the first to form a plus sign.

8. Transfer the dough to the baking stone and bake for 30 minutes.

9. The bread is ready when tapping on the bottom produces a hollow sound. Store the bread in an airtight container at room temperature for up to 2 days. If you wish to store the bread longer, store it in the freezer in a sealed freezer bag for up to 1 week. To reheat, defrost at room temperature and place in a 400°F oven for 6 minutes.

# BREAD STUFFED WITH OLIVES AND CHEESE

*This delicious recipe is not difficult to make but is very difficult to put down once you've tasted it.*

## INGREDIENTS

*Serves 4*

For the dough:

1 cup cold water

1 tablespoon dried yeast

3 cups bread flour

2 tablespoons olive oil

1 teaspoon salt

Flour for dusting

For the filling:

$\frac{2}{3}$ cup pitted green olives

$\frac{1}{2}$ cup mozzarella cheese, grated

$\frac{1}{4}$ cup blue cheese, crumbled

## PREPARATION

1. Place the water, yeast, flour, and olive oil in a mixing bowl. Use an electric mixer with a kneading hook to mix the dough on low speed for 3 minutes.

2. Add the salt while kneading. Increase the mixing speed and continue to knead for 8 minutes.

3. Transfer the dough to a floured bowl, cover with a towel, and let stand to rise at room temperature for 1 hour, until the dough doubles in size.

4. When the dough has risen, transfer to a floured work surface. Use a floured rolling pin to roll out the dough $\frac{1}{2}$-inch thick.

5. Evenly distribute the olives and cheeses on the dough. Roll the dough into a cylinder with the filling inside. Be careful to fold the corners of the dough inward while rolling to keep the filling inside.

6. Place the bread on a baking sheet lined with parchment paper and set aside to rise for 1 hour until the bread has doubled in size.

7. Preheat the oven to 400°F.

8. Bake for 35 minutes. Remove the bread from the oven and transfer to a cooling rack to cool for 15 minutes before serving. Store the bread in an airtight container at room temperature for up to 2 days. If you wish to store the bread longer, store it in the freezer in a sealed freezer bag for up to 1 week. To reheat, defrost at room temperature and place in a 400°F oven for 6 minutes.

# WHOLE WHEAT OLIVE BREAD

*This surprisingly light yet filling bread goes great with hearty lunchtime fare.*
*It's also perfect for just munching on with your favorite glass of wine.*

## INGREDIENTS

*Serves 4*

1 cup cold water

1 tablespoon dried yeast

3 cups whole wheat flour

⅔ cup pitted black olives in wine, drained

1 teaspoon salt

Flour for dusting

## PREPARATION

1. Place the water, yeast, flour, and olives in a mixing bowl. Use an electric mixer with a kneading hook to mix the dough on low speed for 3 minutes.

2. Add the salt while kneading. Increase the mixing speed and continue to knead for 6 minutes.

3. Transfer the dough to a floured bowl, cover with a towel, and let stand to rise at room temperature for 1 hour until the dough doubles in size.

4. When the dough has risen, transfer it to a floured work surface. Form a ball, and then roll the ball into a loaf shape about 12 inches long.

5. Place the loaf on a baking sheet lined with parchment paper and sprinkle flour generously over the loaf. Let stand to rise for 1 hour.

6. Preheat the oven to 400°F.

7. Just before placing the bread in the oven, use a sharp knife to score a line lengthwise across the top of the loaf.

8. Place in the oven and bake for 30 minutes. The bread is ready when tapping on the bottom produces a hollow sound. Store the bread in an airtight container at room temperature for up to 2 days. If you wish to store the bread longer, store it in the freezer in a sealed freezer bag for up to 1 week. To reheat, defrost at room temperature and place in a 400°F oven for 6 minutes.

# TURKISH OLIVE PASTRIES

*These delicious stuffed filo coils are one of the many shaped* borek *(pastries)*
*served in Turkey.*

## INGREDIENTS

*Serves 6*

½ cup pitted black olives,
coarsely chopped

½ cup cream cheese

⅓ cup kashkaval cheese, grated

1 pound filo dough

¼ cup olive oil

## PREPARATION

1. Preheat the oven to 400°F.

2. Place the olives and cheeses in
a bowl and mix well using a fork.

3. Place the sheets of filo dough
on a clean and dry work surface.
Separate half the olive oil and
brush each sheet of dough
with oil.

4. Cut the filo into 4-inch by
2-inch rectangles.

5. Spoon a ½-inch by 3-inch
rectangle of filling in the center
of each piece of filo.

6. Coil each filo piece into a
4-inch-diameter wheel.

7. Place the wheels onto a baking
sheet lined with parchment paper
and coat each wheel with the rest
of the olive oil.

8. Bake for 14 minutes.

9. Serve hot. Store in the
refrigerator for up to 24 hours
and reheat in a 400°F oven for
4–5 minutes.

# FOCACCIA WITH OLIVES AND ANCHOVIES

*The name* focaccia *is taken from the Latin* panis focacius, *which referred to a flat loaf of bread cooked upon a hearth. Professional bakers often puncture the bread with a knife to relieve bubbling on the surface.*

## INGREDIENTS

*Serves 4*

1 cup cold water

1 tablespoon dry yeast

3 cups bread flour

1/4 cup olive oil

1 tablespoon sugar

1 teaspoon salt

3 tablespoons olive oil

1/2 cup pitted green olives

12 anchovy fillets, pickled in salt

2 tablespoons fresh rosemary

Flour for dusting

## PREPARATION

1. Place the water, yeast, flour, olive oil, and sugar in a mixing bowl. Use an electric mixer with a kneading hook to knead the dough on low speed for 3 minutes. Add the salt, increase the mixing speed to medium, and continue to knead for 6 minutes.

2. Transfer the dough to a floured bowl, cover with a towel, and let stand to rise at room temperature for 1 hour until the dough doubles in size.

3. Transfer the dough to a floured work surface and roll it out 1/2-inch thick. Grease a baking sheet with 1 tablespoon of olive oil and transfer the dough to the baking sheet.

4. Press and stretch the dough with your fingers so that it fits the baking sheet. Set aside for 1 hour to rise until the dough doubles in size.

5. Preheat the oven to 400°F.

6. When the dough has risen, sprinkle the olives, anchovies, and rosemary over the top. Press indentations in the dough where there are no toppings, and pour the remaining 2 tablespoons of olive oil over the focaccia.

7. Bake for 20 minutes. Serve hot. Store in the refrigerator for up to 24 hours and reheat in a 400°F oven for 4–5 minutes.

# GOAT CHEESE AND OLIVE PASTRIES

*Another variety of tasty pastry stuffed with olives and cheese.*
*Use fresh-from-the-farm cheese to maximize the flavor.*

## INGREDIENTS

*Serves 6*

1/2 cup pitted black olives, coarsely chopped

1/2 cup aged goat cheese, crumbled

1/3 cup soft goat cheese

1 pound frozen puff pastry

1 egg, beaten

## PREPARATION

1. Preheat the oven to 400°F.

2. Place the olives and cheeses in a bowl and mix well.

3. Gently roll out the puff pastry on a floured work surface to an 18-inch by 8-inch rectangle. Spoon on the filling mixture and spread it out to cover the pastry. Leave a small border of pastry to prevent the filling from spilling out when rolled. Roll the pastry into a long cylinder and use a sharp knife to cut the cylinder into 1/2-inch slices.

4. Place the pastries on a baking sheet lined with parchment paper. Generously brush each pastry with the beaten egg and bake for 14 minutes. Serve hot. Store in the refrigerator for up to 24 hours and reheat in a 400°F oven for 4–5 minutes.

# OLIVE PUFF PASTRY

*Stuffed with tantalizing olives and creamy cheese, these delightful golden brown pockets of luscious pastry make the perfect appetizer.*

## INGREDIENTS

*Serves 6*

½ cup pitted green olives, coarsely chopped

⅓ cup cream cheese

½ cup feta cheese, crumbled

1 pound frozen puff pastry

1 egg, beaten

## PREPARATION

1. Preheat the oven to 400°F.

2. Place the olives, cream cheese, and feta cheese in a bowl and mix well.

3. Gently roll out the puff pastry on a floured work surface to an 18-inch by 12-inch rectangle. Use a sharp knife to cut out 3-inch squares from the pastry.

4. Spoon a small mound of filling in the center of each pastry square. Fold the corners of the pastry inward and squeeze the pastry gently with your fingers to seal.

5. Place the pastries on a baking sheet lined with parchment paper. Generously brush each one with the beaten egg and bake for 14 minutes. Serve hot. Store in the refrigerator for up to 24 hours and reheat in a 400°F oven for 4–5 minutes.

# PIZZA WITH OLIVE AND TOMATO SPREAD

*A classic pizza recipe that will delight children and adults alike.*

## INGREDIENTS

*Serves 4*

For the dough:

½ cup cold water

½ cup milk

1 tablespoon dried yeast

3 cups bread flour

2 tablespoons olive oil

1 teaspoon salt

Flour for dusting

1 tablespoon olive oil

For the topping:

¼ cup Green Olive Tapenade (page 26)

3 tomatoes, blanched and pureed

½ cup mozzarella cheese, grated

¼ cup pitted black olives

1 teaspoon fresh oregano

1 teaspoon fresh thyme

## PREPARATION

1. Place the water, milk, yeast, flour, and 2 tablespoons olive oil into a mixing bowl. Use an electric mixer with a kneading hook to knead the dough on low speed for 3 minutes. Add the salt, increase the mixing speed to medium, and continue to knead for 9 minutes.

2. Transfer the dough to a floured bowl, cover with a towel, and let stand to rise at room temperature for 1 hour until the dough doubles in size.

3. Transfer the dough to a floured work surface and divide into 4 equal portions. Roll out each portion ¼-inch thick.

4. Grease 2 baking sheets with 1 tablespoon of olive oil. Place 2 portions of dough on each baking sheet and set aside to rise for 30 minutes.

5. Preheat the oven to 450°F.

6. Place the tapenade and the tomatoes in a bowl and mix well.

7. When the dough has risen, spread the olive mixture on top of each portion. Sprinkle the mozzarella cheese on top, then the olives, then the spices.

8. Bake for 15 minutes and serve hot. Store in the refrigerator for up to 24 hours and reheat in a 400°F oven for 4–5 minutes.

# RICE
# AND
# PASTA

# FRIED RICE WITH GREEN OLIVES

*This recipe makes an excellent appetizer or vegetarian side dish.*

## INGREDIENTS

*Serves 4*

3 tablespoons olive oil

1 white onion, finely chopped

2 carrots, cut into $\frac{1}{8}$-inch-wide, 1-inch-long strips

2 celery stalks, thinly sliced

1 clove garlic, chopped

2 cups steamed rice (preferably leftover cooked rice)

$\frac{1}{2}$ cup pitted green olives, halved

1 teaspoon salt

1 teaspoon ground black pepper

1 tablespoon lemon juice, freshly squeezed

## PREPARATION

1. Heat a large skillet over high heat. Place the olive oil and onion in the skillet and sauté until the onion is translucent.

2. Add the carrots, celery, and garlic, and cook for 2 minutes while stirring.

3. Add the rice, olives, salt, and pepper, and cook while stirring for 6 minutes.

4. Add the lemon juice and stir well. Remove from heat and transfer to serving plates. Serve immediately.

# SPAGHETTI WITH TUNA AND OLIVES

*In Italian* spaghetti con tonno, *this dish uses tuna in olive oil to add an extra dimension to this dynamic sauce. Be sure to cook the pasta* al dente *for the best results.*

## INGREDIENTS

*Serves 4*

8 cups water

2 tablespoons olive oil

2 tablespoons coarse salt

One 16-ounce package spaghetti

½ cup Black Olive Tapenade (page 26)

Half 6-ounce can tuna in oil, flaked well with a fork

1 tablespoon lemon juice, freshly squeezed

2 tablespoons parsley, finely chopped

½ teaspoon salt

½ teaspoon ground black pepper

3 tablespoons Parmesan cheese, grated

## PREPARATION

1. Bring the water, 1 tablespoon olive oil, and coarse salt to a boil over high heat.

2. Add the spaghetti and cook for 8 minutes until the spaghetti is *al dente*.

3. Place the tapenade, tuna, lemon juice, parsley, salt, pepper, and Parmesan cheese in a large bowl and mix well.

4. Drain the spaghetti in a colander and pour the remaining olive oil on top. Toss well to coat.

5. Transfer the pasta to the bowl with the tuna and mix well.

6. Arrange on individual serving dishes and serve immediately.

# CHICKEN OLIVE RISOTTO

*For an even tastier risotto, substitute chicken stock for the water*
*and soup powder.*

## INGREDIENTS

*Serves 4*

1 white onion, finely chopped

1 clove garlic, finely chopped

2 tablespoons olive oil

$\frac{1}{2}$ pound white chicken with skin, chopped

$\frac{1}{2}$ cup pitted green olives, finely chopped

$\frac{1}{2}$ cup white wine

1$\frac{1}{2}$ cups arborio rice

$\frac{1}{2}$ cup cherry tomatoes, quartered

1 tablespoon chicken soup powder

2$\frac{1}{2}$ cups boiling water

1 teaspoon salt

1 teaspoon ground white pepper

$\frac{1}{4}$ cup parsley, finely chopped

$\frac{1}{4}$ cup Parmesan cheese, grated

## PREPARATION

1. Heat a wide shallow pan over medium heat. Add the onion, garlic, and olive oil, and sauté for 5 minutes, until the onion is golden brown.

2. Add the chicken and olives and cook for 5 minutes while stirring.

3. Add the white wine and cook for 3 minutes. Add the rice and mix well.

4. Add the cherry tomatoes, soup powder, and 1 cup of boiling water and cook for 10 minutes while stirring.

5. Add the salt, pepper, and 1 cup of boiling water, and cook for 7 minutes while stirring. Add the remaining boiling water and cook for 3 minutes.

6. Add the parsley and half the Parmesan cheese and mix well. Transfer the risotto to a serving dish.

7. Sprinkle the remaining Parmesan cheese on top and serve immediately.

# PENNE WITH BROCCOLI AND GREEN OLIVES

*When cooking the broccoli for this recipe, be careful not to overcook. It should be bright green and only slightly tender.*

## INGREDIENTS

*Serves 4*

12 cups water

2 tablespoons coarse salt

$\frac{1}{2}$ pound broccoli

$\frac{1}{2}$ cup pitted green olives, coarsely chopped

3 tablespoons olive oil

1 tablespoon lemon juice, freshly squeezed

$\frac{1}{2}$ teaspoon salt

$\frac{1}{2}$ teaspoon ground white pepper

One 16-ounce package penne pasta

$\frac{1}{2}$ cup ricotta cheese, crumbled

## PREPARATION

1. Bring the water and the coarse salt to a boil over high heat.

2. When the water is boiling, add the broccoli and cook for about 4 minutes.

3. Remove the broccoli from the water with a slotted spoon and transfer to a large bowl.

4. Add the olives, olive oil, lemon juice, salt, and pepper, and mix well.

5. Add the uncooked pasta to the boiling water and cook over low heat for 12 minutes.

6. Drain the pasta and add to the other ingredients. Mix well and transfer to plates to serve.

7. Sprinkle ricotta cheese over each serving and serve immediately.

# SPAGHETTI WITH TAPENADE

*Prepare the Black Olive Tapenade in advance and have it ready for quick dishes like this one to serve at a moment's notice.*

## INGREDIENTS

*Serves 4*

8 cups water

3 tablespoons olive oil

2 tablespoons coarse salt

One 16-ounce package spaghettini

⅓ cup Black Olive Tapenade (page 26)

¼ cup Parmesan cheese, grated

## PREPARATION

1. Bring the water, 1 tablespoon of olive oil, and coarse salt to a boil over high heat. When the water is boiling, add the pasta, and cook for 8 minutes until the pasta is ready.

2. Place the tapenade and Parmesan cheese in a large bowl.

3. Drain the pasta in a colander and pour the remaining olive oil over the pasta. Toss the pasta to coat. Add to the tapenade and cheese, and mix well.

4. Transfer to individual serving dishes and serve immediately.

# PASTA WITH MUSHROOMS AND OLIVES

*In this heavenly dish, the fresh mushrooms provide a sweet, earthy taste which contrasts strikingly with the tartness of the green olives.*

## INGREDIENTS

*Serves 4*

8 cups water

3 tablespoons olive oil

2 tablespoons coarse salt

One 16-ounce package fusilli pasta

½ pound fresh mushrooms, coarsely chopped

1 clove garlic, chopped

⅓ cup white wine

½ cup pitted black olives, finely chopped

½ teaspoon salt

½ teaspoon ground black pepper

⅓ cup butter

¼ cup Parmesan cheese, grated

## PREPARATION

1. Bring the water, 1 tablespoon of olive oil, and coarse salt to a boil over high heat.

2. When the water comes to a boil, add the pasta, reduce the heat, and cook for 8 minutes until the pasta is cooked. Drain.

3. While the pasta is cooking, prepare the sauce. Heat a heavy skillet over medium heat. Add the mushrooms, garlic, and 2 tablespoons of olive oil, and cook for 5 minutes while stirring.

4. Add the wine and cook for 5 minutes.

5. Add the olives, salt, and pepper, mix well, and cook for 3 minutes.

6. Add the butter and cook while stirring until the butter melts.

7. Transfer the pasta to a large serving dish and pour the sauce on top. Add half the Parmesan cheese and mix well.

8. Transfer to individual dishes and sprinkle each portion with the remaining cheese. Serve immediately.

# PASTA SALAD WITH OLIVES AND SUN-DRIED TOMATOES

*This is a wonderful dish to bring to a pot-luck brunch or to serve at a summer barbeque.*

## INGREDIENTS

*Serves 4*

8 cups water

1 tablespoon olive oil

2 tablespoons coarse salt

½ pound shell-shaped pasta

½ cup pitted black olives

½ cup cherry tomatoes, halved

⅔ cup sun-dried tomatoes in oil, drained with oil reserved and cut into strips

⅓ cup oil drained from tomatoes

1 tablespoon fresh oregano, finely chopped

1 tablespoon lemon juice, freshly squeezed

2 cloves garlic, chopped

8 large fresh basil leaves, cut into strips

½ teaspoon salt

½ teaspoon ground black pepper

## PREPARATION

1. Bring water, olive oil, and salt to a boil over high heat.

2. When the water is boiling, add the pasta and cook for 8 minutes until done. Drain the pasta.

3. Place the olives, both kinds of tomatoes, oil from the tomatoes, oregano, garlic, lemon juice, basil, salt, and pepper in a large bowl and mix well. Add the pasta.

4. Mix well and serve immediately.

# SEAFOOD RISOTTO

*As with most recipes, the fresher the ingredients, the seafood in particular, the tastier the results.*

## INGREDIENTS

*Serves 4*

1 white onion, finely chopped

1 clove garlic, finely chopped

3 tablespoons olive oil

³⁄₄ cup calamari, rings or strips

½ cup pitted black olives, halved

1 cup white wine

1½ cups arborio rice

½ pound cherry tomatoes, blanched

2 small crabs

2 tablespoons chicken soup powder

2½ cups boiling water

1 teaspoon salt

½ teaspoon ground white pepper

1 cup cleaned shrimp

## PREPARATION

1. Heat a wide, shallow pan over medium heat. Add the onion, garlic, and olive oil, and sauté for 5 minutes until the onion is golden brown.

2. Add the calamari and olives and cook for 2 minutes while stirring.

3. Add the white wine and cook for 3 minutes. Add the rice and mix well.

4. Add the tomatoes, crabs, soup powder, and 1 cup of boiling water, and cook for 10 minutes while stirring.

5. Add the salt, pepper, and 1 cup of boiling water, and cook for 7 minutes while stirring.

6. Add the shrimp and ½ cup of boiling water and cook for 3 minutes while stirring.

7. Transfer to individual serving plates and serve immediately.

# PASTA WITH OLIVES AND SUN-DRIED TOMATOES

*The fusion of flavors in this impressive dish will make your taste buds explode.*

## INGREDIENTS

*Serves 4*

8 cups water

1 tablespoon olive oil

2 tablespoons coarse salt

½ pound penne pasta

½ cup pitted black olives

⅔ cup sun-dried tomatoes in oil, drained with oil reserved and cut into strips

⅓ cup oil from tomatoes

⅓ cup olive oil

8 large fresh basil leaves, cut into strips

½ teaspoon salt

½ teaspoon ground black pepper

## PREPARATION

1. Bring the water, olive oil, and salt to a boil over high heat.

2. When the water comes to a boil, add the pasta, reduce the heat, and cook for 8 minutes, until the pasta is cooked. Drain.

3. Place the olives, tomatoes, oils, basil, salt, and pepper in a large bowl and mix well. Add the pasta and mix well.

4. Serve immediately.

# CANNELLONI STUFFED WITH LAMB AND OLIVES

*Though you can certainly purchase uncooked cannelloni in most supermarkets, preparing it yourself with fresh lasagna noodles will create a delightful, impressive dish.*

## INGREDIENTS

*Serves 4*

For the filling:

1 tablespoon olive oil

1 onion, finely chopped

1 pound lamb, chopped

1 clove garlic, finely chopped

1/2 teaspoon salt

1/2 teaspoon ground black pepper

1 tablespoon fresh thyme

For the sauce:

2 tablespoons olive oil

1 clove garlic, finely chopped

1 cup cherry tomatoes, puréed

1/2 cup pitted green olives, coarsely chopped

1 teaspoon salt

1/2 teaspoon ground white pepper

1 cup sweet cream

8 fresh lasagna noodles, cut into 6-inch squares

1 tablespoon olive oil for greasing pan

## PREPARATION

1. Prepare the filling. Heat a large skillet over medium heat. Place the olive oil and onion in the skillet and sauté for 5 minutes. Add the lamb and garlic, and cook while stirring until the lamb is evenly browned.

2. Add the salt, pepper, and thyme, and mix well. Remove from heat and set aside.

3. Prepare the sauce. Heat the olive oil and garlic in a medium saucepan over low heat. Sauté for 2 minutes.

4. Add the cherry tomatoes, olives, salt, and pepper, and cook for 8 minutes.

5. Add the sweet cream and bring to a boil over low heat. Cook for 10 minutes.

6. Prepare the lasagna noodles following manufacturer's instructions. Preheat the oven to 400°F.

7. Lay out the lasagna noodles on a clean, dry work surface.

8. Spoon the filling evenly onto each pasta square. Arrange the filling in a line down the middle of each square from end to end.

9. Roll each square into a cylinder from bottom to top and place the rolls side-by-side in a greased baking dish. Pour the sauce over the pasta.

10. Bake for 30 minutes and serve immediately.

# PASTA WITH SEAFOOD, TOMATOES, AND BLACK OLIVES

*In lieu of calamari, you may use octopus or cuttlefish to produce a truly spectacular meal.*

## INGREDIENTS

*Serves 4*

8 cups water

5 tablespoons olive oil

2 teaspoons coarse salt

One 8-ounce package pasta shells

1 white onion, finely chopped

1 clove garlic, finely chopped

6 large tomatoes, peeled and chopped (or half a large can)

6 ounces calamari, cut into strips

1/4 cup white wine

4 crabs, quartered

1 teaspoon salt

1 teaspoon ground white pepper

1/2 cup pitted black olives, coarsely chopped

7 ounces shrimp, cleaned and peeled

2 tablespoons fresh basil

## PREPARATION

1. Bring the water, 2 tablespoons of olive oil, and coarse salt to a boil over high heat. Reduce heat when water is boiling.

2. Add the pasta and cook for 8 minutes until cooked. Drain the pasta and return to the pot.

3. While the pasta is cooking, prepare the sauce. Heat a heavy skillet over medium heat. Add the onion, garlic, and 3 tablespoons of olive oil, and sauté for 3 minutes while stirring.

4. Add the tomatoes and calamari and cook for 5 minutes while stirring.

5. Add the white wine, crabs, salt, and pepper, and cook for 7 minutes.

6. Add the olives and cook for 8 minutes.

7. Add the shrimp and mix well.

8. Transfer the pasta to a large bowl and pour the sauce over it. Add the basil and mix well.

9. Transfer to individual serving dishes and serve immediately.

# PENNE TOSCANA

*This quick and easy pasta dish is ideal for a midweek family dinner or for weekend entertaining. Using leftover or store-bought roast chicken makes this pasta dish even easier.*

## INGREDIENTS

*Serves 6*

8 cups water

5 tablespoons olive oil

2 tablespoons coarse salt

One 16-ounce package penne pasta

1 clove garlic, chopped

2 medium-size tomatoes, minced

½ cup pitted black olives, coarsely chopped

1 cup white wine

1 pound roast chicken meat (store-bought or leftover)

½ teaspoon salt

½ teaspoon ground black pepper

1 tablespoon fresh basil, coarsely chopped

¼ cup Parmesan cheese

## PREPARATION

1. Bring the water, 2 tablespoons of olive oil, and coarse salt to a boil over high heat.

2. When the water comes to a boil, add the pasta, reduce the heat, and cook for 8 minutes, until the pasta is cooked. Drain the pasta and return to the pot.

3. While the pasta is cooking, prepare the sauce. Heat a heavy skillet over medium heat. Add the garlic and 3 tablespoons of olive oil, and sauté for 2 minutes while stirring.

4. Add the tomatoes and olives and cook for 5 minutes.

5. Add the white wine and chicken and cook for 5 minutes.

6. Add the salt, pepper, and basil, and mix well.

7. Transfer to a large serving bowl, add the pasta and half the Parmesan cheese, and mix well.

8. Transfer to individual serving dishes and sprinkle the remaining Parmesan cheese over each portion. Serve immediately.

# BEEFY OLIVE RISOTTO

*This mouthwatering recipe is a great favorite among children.*

## INGREDIENTS

*Serves 4*

1 pound chopped beef

3 tablespoons olive oil

1 onion, finely chopped

1 carrot diced

2 celery stalks, thinly sliced

1 teaspoon salt

$\frac{1}{2}$ teaspoon ground black pepper

1 $\frac{1}{2}$ cups arborio rice

$\frac{1}{2}$ cup pitted black olives, coarsely chopped

1 tablespoon tomato paste

$\frac{1}{2}$ cup white wine

2 cups boiling water

1 tablespoon chicken soup powder

$\frac{1}{4}$ cup Parmesan cheese, grated

## PREPARATION

1. Heat a medium saucepan over medium heat. When the pan is hot, place the meat and oil in the pan and cook for 15 minutes while stirring.

2. Add the onion, carrot, celery, salt, and pepper, and continue to cook for 10 minutes, while stirring, until the vegetables are just tender.

3. Add the rice, olives, tomato paste, and wine, and mix well. Cook for 3 minutes.

4. Add the boiling water and soup powder and reduce the heat. Continue to cook for 15 minutes while stirring.

5. Check the rice for doneness. If the rice is not soft, cook for 3 more minutes while stirring.

6. Sprinkle the cheese on top and serve hot.

# CHICKEN AND BEEF PAELLA WITH OLIVES

*The name* paella *comes from the Valencian word for "frying pan." The dish originated in Valencia, Spain, and is still a traditional meal eaten during the Falles festival in that part of the world.*

## INGREDIENTS

*Serves 4*

2 tablespoons olive oil

½ pound ribsteak, cut into 2-inch cubes

6 white chicken thighs

1 white onion, finely chopped

1 clove garlic, chopped

1 cup cherry tomatoes, halved

1 teaspoon salt

1 teaspoon ground black pepper

1½ cups long-grained or jasmine rice

½ cup pitted black olives

1 teaspoon paprika

½ cup white wine

2 cups sun-dried tomatoes in oil, finely chopped

2 cups boiling water

## PREPARATION

1. Preheat the oven to 400°F.

2. Heat a deep skillet or shallow pan over medium heat. Add the olive oil, beef, and chicken thighs, and cook for 5 minutes until the meat is browned. Turn while cooking to brown evenly on all sides.

3. Add the onion and garlic, and cook until the onions are golden brown.

4. Add the cherry tomatoes, salt, and pepper, and cook until the liquid is thickened.

5. Add the rice, olives, paprika, and wine, and cook for 2 minutes.

6. Add the sun-dried tomatoes and boiling water, and mix well. Place the chicken thighs on top of the paella as shown in the photo.

7. Bake in the oven for 17 minutes.

8. Serve hot.

# PASTA WITH BEEF AND OLIVE SAUCE

*Lean ground beef produces optimal results in this flavorful recipe. Fattier beef will make the sauce too heavy.*

## INGREDIENTS

*Serves 4*

8 cups water

3 tablespoons olive oil

2 tablespoons coarse salt

One 16-ounce package short pasta (any kind)

1 white onion, finely chopped

2 cloves garlic, chopped

½ pound lean ground beef, chopped

½ cup red wine

1 tablespoon fresh thyme

½ teaspoon salt

½ teaspoon ground white pepper

½ cup pitted black olives

1 cup cherry tomatoes, halved

## PREPARATION

1. Bring the water, 1 tablespoon of olive oil, and the coarse salt to a boil over high heat. When the water has boiled, reduce the heat.

2. When the water comes to a boil, add the pasta, reduce the heat, and cook for 8 minutes until the pasta is ready. Drain pasta and set aside.

3. While the pasta is cooking, prepare the sauce. Heat a heavy skillet over medium heat. Add the onion, garlic, and 2 tablespoons of olive oil and sauté for 5 minutes while stirring.

4. Add the chopped beef and cook for 10 minutes.

5. Add the wine, thyme, salt, and pepper, and cook for 5 minutes.

6. Add the olives and cherry tomatoes and cook for 8 minutes.

7. Transfer the pasta to a large bowl and pour the sauce over it. Mix well.

8. Transfer to individual serving dishes and serve immediately.

# SPAGHETTI WITH RICOTTA AND BLACK OLIVES

*Fresh ricotta cheese gives the sauce for this recipe a light and creamy texture.*

## INGREDIENTS

*Serves 4*

12 cups water

3 tablespoons olive oil

2 tablespoons coarse salt

One 16-ounce package spaghetti

$\frac{1}{2}$ cup pitted black olives, coarsely chopped

2 tablespoons fresh basil, coarsely chopped

$\frac{1}{2}$ tablespoon lemon juice, freshly squeezed

1 teaspoon salt

$\frac{3}{4}$ cup fresh ricotta cheese

1. Bring the water, 1 tablespoon of olive oil, and salt to a boil over high heat. When the water is boiling, add the spaghetti and cook for 8 minutes until ready.

2. While the pasta is cooking, place the olives, basil, lemon juice, and salt in a large bowl and mix well.

3. When the pasta is done, drain and pour the remaining olive oil over the pasta. Mix well and transfer to the bowl with the olive mixture. Add half the ricotta and mix well.

4. Arrange the pasta on serving plates and crumble the remaining ricotta on top. Serve immediately.

# FISH AND
# SEAFOOD

# SPICED OLIVE MONKFISH CASSEROLE

*If you can't find monkfish meat for this recipe, you may substitute with lobster, red snapper, or shark.*

## INGREDIENTS

*Serves 4*

2 pounds monkfish, sliced 1-inch thick

1 cup pitted black olives, finely chopped

2 cloves garlic, finely chopped

1/4 cup olive oil

1 tablespoon fresh thyme

1 teaspoon coriander

1 teaspoon whole cumin seeds

1/2 teaspoon ground black pepper

1 teaspoon coarse salt

## PREPARATION

1. Preheat the oven to 400°F.

2. Place all the ingredients in a large bowl and mix well.

3. Transfer to a deep casserole dish and cook, covered, for 20 minutes.

4. After 20 minutes, uncover and cook for 5 more minutes.

5. Remove from the oven and serve immediately. Store in the refrigerator for up to 2 days. Reheat before serving.

# CUTTLEFISH AND OLIVE CASSEROLE

*Cuttlefish adds a delicious marine flavor and smoothness to this excellent seafood casserole.*

## INGREDIENTS

*Serves 4*

2 pounds cuttlefish, cleaned

1/2 cup pitted green olives, coarsely chopped

3 tomatoes, blanched and cut into 1/2-inch cubes

1 teaspoon rosemary

2 cloves garlic, finely chopped

1 teaspoon coarse salt

1/2 teaspoon ground white pepper

1/2 cup white wine

1/4 cup olive oil

## PREPARATION

1. Preheat the oven to 400°F.

2. Place the cuttlefish, olives, tomatoes, rosemary, garlic, salt, and pepper in a large bowl and mix well.

3. Transfer to a deep casserole dish. Add the wine and olive oil.

4. Cover the dish and cook, covered, for 50 minutes.

5. Uncover and cook for 20 more minutes.

6. Remove from oven and serve immediately. Store in the refrigerator for up to 2 days. Reheat before serving.

# SHRIMP IN TOMATO OLIVE SAUCE

*It is important to cook shrimp properly. When ready, it will be opaque and pearly white.*

## INGREDIENTS

*Serves 4*

2 cloves garlic, finely chopped

3 tablespoons olive oil

½ cup pitted green olives, coarsely chopped

5 tomatoes, blanched and pureed

½ teaspoon salt

½ teaspoon ground white pepper

1½ pounds shrimp, heads removed, peeled and cleaned

1 tablespoon fresh basil, chopped

## PREPARATION

1. Heat a large skillet over medium heat. Add the garlic and olive oil and sauté for 1 minute.

2. Add the olives and tomatoes and mix well. Reduce heat and cook for 15 minutes.

3. Add the salt and pepper, and mix well. Check the consistency of the sauce. If it hasn't thickened, cook for 5 more minutes.

4. Add the shrimp and cook for 2 minutes on each side. Remove from heat.

5. Add the basil and mix well.

6. Transfer to a serving dish and serve immediately.

# OLIVE-CRUSTED FILLET OF SEA BASS

*When selecting fish for cooking, look for clear eyes, red gills, and moist shiny skin. If the fish is already filleted, look for firm flesh that is closely packed and not ragged.*

## INGREDIENTS

*Serves 4*

Two 1-pound sea bass fillets, cleaned

½ cup pitted green olives, finely chopped

½ cup breadcrumbs

3 tablespoons olive oil

1 tablespoon fresh thyme

1 clove garlic, finely chopped

½ teaspoon coarse salt

½ teaspoon ground black pepper

2 tablespoons lemon juice, freshly squeezed

## PREPARATION

1. Preheat the oven to 450°F.

2. Cut each fillet in half and place skin-side up in a shallow baking dish lined with parchment paper.

3. Place the olives, breadcrumbs, olive oil, thyme, garlic, salt, and pepper in a medium bowl.

4. Mix well until the mixture is the consistency of wet sand.

5. Spread the breadcrumb mixture completely over the fish.

6. Bake for 10 minutes.

7. Remove from the oven and arrange on a serving dish. Pour the lemon juice over the fish and serve immediately.

# TUNA STEAK IN GREEN OLIVE SAUCE

*Raw tuna steak looks similar to raw beef and should be a deep red color. The tuna steak may have a darker brown area which is edible but has a much stronger flavor.*

## INGREDIENTS

*Serves 2*

1/3 cup pitted green olives, coarsely chopped

2 tablespoons capers, finely chopped

1 teaspoon white wine vinegar

3 tablespoons olive oil

1 pound fresh tuna, halved

1/2 teaspoon coarse salt

1/2 teaspoon ground black pepper

2 handfuls baby salad greens

## PREPARATION

1. Place the olives, capers, vinegar, and olive oil in a large bowl, and mix well.

2. Heat a Teflon skillet over medium heat.

3. Sprinkle salt and pepper over both sides of the tuna.

4. Place the tuna in the skillet without oil and cook for 3 minutes on each side.

5. Transfer the tuna to two serving plates, and garnish with some of the salad greens on the side. Spoon 2/3 of the sauce on the top while the fish is still warm so that it absorbs the flavor. Pour the remaining sauce over the salad greens and serve immediately.

# SHRIMP AND OLIVE STIR-FRY

*Simple, yet extraordinarily tasty, this seafood stir-fry can be whipped up for a late-night supper or when surprise guests arrive.*

## INGREDIENTS

*Serves 4*

1½ pounds large shrimp, heads removed, peeled and cleaned

½ cup pitted black olives, coarsely chopped

3 tablespoons olive oil

3 cloves garlic, coarsely chopped

½ teaspoon ground black pepper

½ teaspoon salt

1 tablespoon lemon juice, freshly squeezed

## PREPARATION

1. Heat a heavy skillet over medium heat. Add the shrimp without oil and grill for 2 minutes on each side.

2. Add the remaining ingredients except for the lemon juice and grill for 3 minutes.

3. Remove from heat and add the lemon juice. Let stand for 5 minutes. Serve immediately.

# BAKED WHOLE SEA BASS IN OLIVE SAUCE

*Serve this fish whole on a bed of greens to create an impressive centerpiece for a light supper or dinner party.*

## INGREDIENTS

*Serves 2*

1½-pound whole sea bass, cleaned

2 cloves garlic, finely sliced

4 sprigs fresh basil

5 sprigs fresh parsley

10 sprigs fresh thyme

1 teaspoon salt

½ teaspoon ground black pepper

1¼ cups olive oil

½ cup pitted black olives, finely chopped

3 tablespoons lemon juice, freshly squeezed

## PREPARATION

1. Preheat the oven to 450°F.

2. Use a sharp knife to cut 3 slices horizontally, along the top of the fish, from head to tail (see photo). In addition, make one slice across the belly of the fish. Place the fish in a baking dish.

3. Arrange the garlic slices vertically in the slices on top of the fish. Place the basil, parsley, and thyme in the belly slice.

4. Sprinkle half the salt and all of the pepper over the fish and in the belly slice. Drizzle 1 tablespoon of olive oil on top of the fish. Bake for 18 minutes.

5. While the fish is baking, place the olives, remaining olive oil, lemon juice, and remaining salt in a medium bowl, and mix well.

6. Remove the fish from the oven and transfer to a serving plate. Pour the sauce over the fish or serve it separately. Serve immediately.

# MUSSELS IN OLIVE SAUCE

*Choosing fresh mussels is important when preparing this dish. Be sure to choose mussels that are tightly closed and not unusually heavy for their size.*

## INGREDIENTS

*Serves 4*

3 tablespoons olive oil

1/4 cup leeks, finely chopped

1/4 cup celery, finely chopped

1 small red onion, finely chopped

1/3 cup carrots, diced

1/2 teaspoon salt

1/2 teaspoon ground white pepper

1/2 cup pitted green olives, thinly sliced

2 pounds fresh mussels

2 cloves garlic, finely chopped

1/2 cup white wine

## PREPARATION

1. Heat a deep pan over medium heat. Make sure the pan is large enough to generously accommodate the ingredients since the mussels open when cooking and double in size. Add the olive oil, leek, celery, onion, carrots, salt, and pepper, and cook until the vegetables are tender.

2. Add the olives, mussels, and garlic and mix well. Pour the wine over the mixture and cover the pan. Cook for 15 minutes.

3. Remove from heat and use a slotted spoon to transfer to a serving dish. Serve immediately.

# RED MULLET IN OLIVE CAPER SAUCE

*Serve this fish with a high-acidity wine, such as a red Anjou or white Burgundy.*

## INGREDIENTS

*Serves 4*

2 pounds medium striped red mullet, cleaned

3 lemons, halved and thinly sliced

$\frac{1}{2}$ teaspoon coarse salt

$\frac{1}{2}$ teaspoon ground black pepper

6 tablespoons olive oil

$\frac{1}{2}$ cup pitted green olives, finely chopped

3 tablespoons Green Olive Tapenade (page 26)

3 tablespoons capers, finely chopped

$\frac{1}{2}$ teaspoon salt

2 tablespoons lemon juice, freshly squeezed

## PREPARATION

1. Preheat the oven to 450°F.

2. Arrange the fish on a baking sheet lined with parchment paper. Place the lemon slices inbetween the fish.

3. Sprinkle coarse salt and pepper over the fish and drizzle 2 tablespoons of olive oil over the fish.

4. Bake for 8 minutes.

5. While the fish is baking, prepare the sauce. Place the olives, tapenade, and capers in a large bowl and mix well. Add the remaining olive oil while mixing. Add the salt and lemon juice and mix well.

6. Remove the fish from the oven, transfer to a serving dish, and pour the sauce over the fish while it is still hot. Serve immediately.

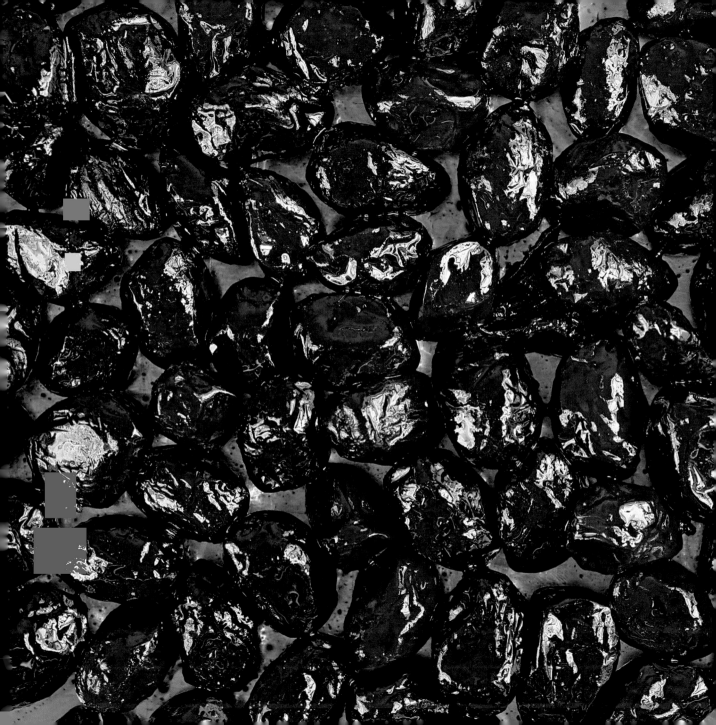

# CHICKEN AND MEAT

# ROASTED CHICKEN THIGHS WITH BLACK OLIVES

*An easy-to-prepare dinner, serve this chicken entrée with wide noodles and a fresh green salad and your family will thank you.*

## INGREDIENTS

*Serves 4*

12 chicken thighs, cleaned

5 medium potatoes, quartered

$\frac{1}{3}$ cup pitted black olives

3 tablespoons olive oil

1 tablespoon fresh oregano

$\frac{1}{2}$ teaspoon ground black pepper

1 teaspoon salt

## PREPARATION

1. Preheat the oven to 400°F.

2. Place all the ingredients in a large bowl and mix well.

3. Transfer to a deep baking dish and cover.

4. Cook for 40 minutes.

5. Uncover and cook for 15 more minutes.

6. The chicken and potatoes should be golden brown. If they aren't, return to the oven for 5 more minutes.

7. Serve hot or store in an airtight container in the refrigerator for up to 2 days. Reheat before serving.

# ESTOUFFAD PROVENÇAL

*An estouffad is a type of stew with slowly simmered ingredients. It is usually made with beef, wine, carrots, and onions.*

## INGREDIENTS

*Serves 4*

¼ cup olive oil

2 pounds beef shoulder, cut into 2-inch cubes

2 carrots, cut into ½-inch cubes

1 onion, finely chopped

2 celery stalks, cut into ¼-inch slices

2 teaspoons salt

1 cup white wine

2 cups red wine

3 cups water

½ cup pitted green olives

3 tablespoons tomato sauce

2 tablespoons flour

1 teaspoon ground white pepper

## PREPARATION

1. Heat a large ovenproof saucepan over medium heat. Add half the olive oil and the beef. Sear the beef briefly until it browns to seal in the juices.

2. Remove the beef and set aside.

3. Without cleaning the pan, add the carrots, onion, celery, remaining olive oil, and 1 teaspoon of salt, and cook until the vegetables are tender.

4. Return the beef to the pan, add the white wine, and cook for 5 minutes.

5. Add the red wine, water, olives, tomato sauce, flour, pepper, and remaining salt, and bring to a boil.

6. Preheat the oven to 400°F.

7. When the mixture comes to a boil, cover the pan and transfer to the oven for 2 hours.

8. Uncover and cook for 20 more minutes.

9. Serve immediately or store in the refrigerator for up to 1 day and reheat before serving.

# CHICKEN BREASTS STUFFED WITH OLIVES

*Elegant and delicious as an entrée for a special occasion.*

## INGREDIENTS

*Serves 4*

1½ pounds chicken breasts, flattened for stuffing

3 tablespoons olive oil

½ teaspoon salt

½ teaspoon ground black pepper

1 cup pitted green olives, coarsely chopped

⅓ cup pitted black olives, coarsely chopped

2 tablespoons fresh parsley, coarsely chopped

2 cloves garlic, finely chopped

3 tablespoons Parmesan cheese, grated

## PREPARATION

1. Preheat the oven to 400°F.

2. Place the chicken, oil, salt, and pepper in a bowl, and mix well. Set aside.

3. In a separate bowl, mix together the olives, parsley, garlic, and Parmesan cheese.

4. Arrange pieces of aluminum foil on a work surface. The aluminum foil pieces should each be slightly larger than the chicken breasts.

5. Place the chicken on the foil and spoon 3 tablespoons of filling into each breast. Roll the chicken into a cylinder like a roulade and close the ends tightly. Wrap the chicken tightly in the foil, and twist the ends like a candy wrapper. Place the wrapped chicken on a baking sheet.

6. Bake for 30 minutes.

7. Remove from the oven and let the chicken cool for 10 minutes to room temperature.

8. Unwrap the chicken and return to the oven for 5 minutes.

9. Remove and transfer to a cutting board. With a sharp knife, slice the chicken into ½ inch thick slices. Arrange on a serving plate and serve immediately.

# LAMB CASSEROLE WITH BLACK OLIVES

*Thick chunks of potato with tender lamb and black olives will delight your taste buds and leave you wanting more.*

## INGREDIENTS

*Serves 4*

1/4 cup olive oil

2 pounds lamb shoulder, cut into 1/2-inch cubes

1 onion, finely chopped

2 carrots, cut into 1/4-inch cubes

2 celery stalks, cut into 1/4-inch slices

2 teaspoons salt

2 cups white wine

1 pound new potatoes, halved

4 cups water

1/2 cup pitted black olives

2 tablespoons tomato sauce

2 tablespoons flour

1 teaspoon ground black pepper

## PREPARATION

1. Heat a large oven-proof pan over medium heat. Add half the olive oil and lightly brown the meat to seal in the juices. Remove the meat and set aside.

2. Without cleaning the pan, add the onion, carrots, celery, remaining oil, and 1 teaspoon of salt, and cook until the vegetables are tender.

3. Add the browned meat and wine and cook for 5 minutes.

4. Add the potatoes, water, olives, tomato sauce, flour, pepper, and remaining salt, and bring to a boil.

5. Preheat the oven to 400°F.

6. When the mixture comes to a boil, cover and place in the oven for 1 hour and 30 minutes.

7. Remove the cover and cook for 20 minutes more.

8. Serve immediately or store in an airtight container in the refrigerator for up to 1 day. Reheat before serving.

# SCALLOPINI IN OLIVE SAUCE

*Adding olives to veal scallopini makes this classic dish even more exquisite.*

## INGREDIENTS

*Serves 4*

3 tablespoons flour

2 pounds veal thinly sliced for scallopini

3 tablespoons olive oil

10 sage leaves

2 cloves garlic, chopped

1 cup white wine

⅓ cup pitted black olives

⅓ cup chilled butter

½ teaspoon salt

½ teaspoon ground white pepper

## PREPARATION

1. Heat a large skillet over medium heat.

2. Place the flour in a deep dish, and dip each slice of veal inside to coat it completely.

3. Add olive oil to the skillet and cook the veal slices for 2 minutes on each side.

4. Remove the veal and set aside. Add the sage and garlic to the skillet and cook for 2 minutes.

5. Add the wine and olives, and cook for 3 minutes over high heat.

6. Add the cooked veal, butter, salt, and pepper, and cook over high heat, stirring until the liquid begins to thicken.

7. Transfer to a serving plate and serve immediately.

# OLIVE-CRUSTED PORK FILLET

*The crispy contrast between the tender pork fillet and the olive and breadcrumb coating creates a dazzlingly delicious entrée.*

## INGREDIENTS

*Serves 4*

⅓ cup pitted black olives, finely chopped

¼ cup breadcrumbs

2 tablespoons olive oil

2 cloves garlic, finely chopped

1 tablespoon fresh thyme

½ teaspoon coarse salt

½ teaspoon ground black pepper

2 pounds pork fillet

2 rosemary sprigs, for garnish

## PREPARATION

1. Preheat the oven to 400°F.

2. Place the olives, breadcrumbs, oil, garlic, thyme, salt, and pepper in a bowl, and mix well.

3. Arrange the pork on a baking sheet lined with parchment paper. Cover the pork with the olive mixture and bake for 15 minutes.

4. Remove from the oven, transfer to a cutting board, and let stand for 5 minutes before cutting. Use a sharp knife to cut the pork into ½-inch slices.

5. Arrange on a serving platter, garnish with rosemary, and serve immediately.

# CHICKEN MEATBALLS WITH OLIVES

*The traditional meatball made with chicken instead of beef is a lighter and healthier alternative. Here, it is enhanced with an extraordinary olive sauce.*

## INGREDIENTS

*Serves 4*

For the sauce:

3 tablespoons olive oil

1 onion, finely chopped

1 cup cherry tomatoes, halved

⅓ cup pitted green olives

½ teaspoon salt

½ teaspoon ground black pepper

For the meatballs:

1½ pounds chopped chicken

1 cup pitted green olives, coarsely chopped

1 egg

⅓ cup breadcrumbs

1 teaspoon salt

½ teaspoon ground white pepper

## PREPARATION

1. To prepare the sauce, heat a large saucepan over medium heat. Add the olive oil and onion, and cook until the onion is golden.

2. Add the tomatoes, olives, salt, and pepper, and cover the pan. Cook over low heat for 30 minutes.

3. While the sauce is cooking, prepare the meatballs. Place the chicken, olives, egg, breadcrumbs, salt, and pepper in a large bowl, and mix well with your hands to uniform consistency.

4. Form 2-inch-round balls and set aside.

5. After the sauce has cooked for 30 minutes, uncover the pan and add the meatballs.

6. Cover the pan and cook for 30 minutes over low heat.

7. Remove from heat and serve immediately, or store in an airtight container in the refrigerator for up to 2 days and reheat before serving.

# OLIVE-STUFFED POUSSIN

*Poussin, also known as spring chicken, coquelet, and Cornish game hen, is a*
*young chicken bred for extra flavor and tenderness.*

## INGREDIENTS

*Serves 4*

1 cup pitted green olives

3 tablespoons olive oil

3 cloves garlic, chopped

1 tablespoon fresh thyme

½ teaspoon ground black pepper

6 sprigs rosemary

1 teaspoon coarse salt

2 Cornish hens, preferably organic

## PREPARATION

1. Preheat the oven to 400°F.

2. Place the olives, oil, garlic, thyme, pepper, 4 rosemary sprigs, and half the salt in a bowl, and mix well.

3. Stuff the hens with the olive mixture. Rub any remaining liquid from the stuffing over the hens. Sprinkle the remaining salt over the hens and place in a deep baking dish.

4. Tie the legs of the hens with cooking twine, and garnish with the remaining rosemary.

5. Bake for 20 minutes, breast-side down. Turn the hens on their sides, cook for another 20 minutes, and repeat for the other side.

6. Serve immediately, or store in an airtight container in the refrigerator for up to 2 days and reheat before serving.

# INDEX